SECOND PLA
POEMS ABO

SECOND PLACE ROSETTE

POEMS ABOUT BRITAIN

Edited by Emma Dai'an Wright
and Richard O'Brien

THE EMMA PRESS

First published in the UK in 2018 by the Emma Press Ltd.

ISBN 978-1-910139-55-4

A CIP catalogue record of this book
is available from the British Library.

Printed and bound in the EU by Pulsio, Paris.

The Emma Press
theemmapress.com
queries@theemmapress.com
Jewellery Quarter, Birmingham, UK

INTRODUCTION

'Britishness' is a battleground, and often it feels like the only thing we can say for certain is that the people who confidently claim to define it are usually talking bollocks.

To some, talking about 'Britain' for any length of time can smack of nationalism, jingoism, imperialism and misty-eyed fascism – all the bad -isms. But for some who have fled trauma to make these shores their home, the dismissal of any idea of national belonging – however arbitrary or fragile, however bound up in destructive institutions – might signal only the privilege of those who have always known where they belonged.

With the isolationism of Brexit looming, we wanted to explore the idea of Britain in a way that allowed for a multitude of interpretations: not denying the shameful aspects of our history, but recognising what we can be proud of. For all its flaws, Britain is the country that offered a better future to our parents and grandparents as immigrants from Ireland and refugees from Vietnam.

For this book, we decided to reject top-down, 'official' images of what it means to be British in favour of a grass-roots understanding of nationhood, borrowing the 'almanac' structure of the *Fasti* – a chronological compendium of Roman beliefs and festivals by the Latin poet Ovid – and concentrating on holidays, customs and rituals.

Our selection process as editors started from the premise that anything can be a ritual, even if it only matters for one family or one person. Dean Atta's 'The Door', for instance, explores the recurring experience of visiting a grandparent who refuses to put the central heating on, while Carolyn O'Connell's 'On July 28th' describes a summer holiday feast with strolling neighbours popping their heads over the garden fence. Over the course of the year we see celebrations and moments of mourning; mehndi painting and Saturday soup; a pub Christmas dinner and the season's aftermath, pine needles glittering on the floor.

What emerged from our submissions is a patchwork quilt of Britishness, made up of many fabrics and textures. We were surprised by some omissions in the work we received: no poets we chose addressed Easter, or Diwali, or St David's Day, as significant customs. But the local focus of many writers brought its own riches: we have poems about snacking at the Sabbath, watching trash TV at Eid, the Abbots Bromley horn dance and the Haxey Hood.

The voices in this book are warm, plural, and distinctively individual. But as a collective, we feel these poets have captured something true and enduring about life on a bit of land shaped by its geography, its weather, and its sometimes painful history.

Emma Dai'an Wright and Richard O'Brien
BIRMINGHAM, OCTOBER 2018

CONTENTS

January

February

March

April

May

November

December

CR

SARAH BARR

Twelfth Night

You unwind the lights.
The carpet crunches with needles
but the tree still looks healthy.

I lift tinsel and unhook baubles,
the mother of pearl star,
milky glass teardrop,
pink raffia people,
Peruvian clay bells,
and homemade fairy cat,

put them all in the box.
Still glitter-dust may linger
tucked in edges behind the sofa.

You drag the tree out, down the path,
chop it in pieces, onto the bonfire,
create festivities of smoke, sparks, flames.

ROB WALTON

The Haxey Hood
Clarifications and Confusions

So I was talking to Russ
about never having seen it
and my parents just a couple of villages away
and we tried piecing the rules together
pleased that there were few
but we came up with *lots of questions.*

In this or that rolling maul,
this ruck in motion and most likely mud,
*who really holds sway and can be swayed
in these parts at this time?*

If the scrum collapses
and people help each other to their feet
as the battle rages, *how much of a hand
offered to others is acceptable
in this place, in this day and age?*

When folk are trying to get this thing
to one local pub or another
where Haxey and Westwoodside people
drink local beer with other locals, *would I be welcome
if I only knew the rules
to other games?*

On the Twelfth Day of Christmas
(only never on a Sunday)
when this moving scrimmage sways
would it be all right to nip off
and take my Christmas tree down?

The hood hangs in the winning pub for the year.
What would happen if someone took it
to another pub
or just took it?

The game may once have been played with a bullock's head.
Did bloody killjoys put paid to that?

If I want answers to these questions
should I ask the Lord, the Fool or the Boggins?

* The Haxey Hood is held in North Lincolnshire on Twelfth Night.
More information at http://www.wheewall.com/hood/

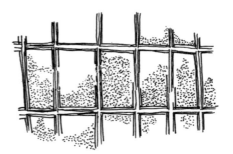

Lighthouse

I never knew how much Yorkshire puddings
were like lighthouses to us land dwellers,
until I heard him speak of voyages,
safe returns, and victories in endings.

He said lighthouses let you know you're home,
let you know you'd made it through the stormy weather.
Made it through the sea chopping
at your boat like mom chopping at potatoes.

Experienced sailors can smell the land
before they can see it; I smell gravy
before I see the chicken. It smells like
glory, survival, family, rest.

I made it. Strong tides couldn't stop my flow.
We rest now. We sail again tomorrow.

Up Helly Aa

Winter on the island, dark and birdless,
and so cold even the seafoam freezes

mid-curl, like a snarled lip. Night on night,
the black streets whistle with a wind that jimmies

collars and keyholes with a thief's knack.
Weeks of banging in the lockups and sheds,

weeks of hammers, wood, and sweat
in the dark hours, with the wee ones in bed

dreaming of half-forgotten colours. And then
the work is done, the boat unloaded

into the bitter Scottish cold, and even the stars
recede in the light of the islanders'

torches. Their sleeves are bright
as they sing their way down to the water.

* Up Helly Aa is a festival celebrated in the Shetlands in
mid-winter. In recognition of their ancestry, the islanders
spend weeks constructing a Viking longship. On the night
of the festival, they wear traditional dress and form a
procession, where they sing the boat down to the water
before setting it on fire.

* The italicised sections of the poem are classic
lines spoken by early Coronation Street characters.

CLAIRE ORCHARD

*Lancashire Blues**

Saturday nights, those first trumpet notes
piping from the beige-fronted TV speaker
the signal to show up and shut up.

Nana and Grandad,
their matching brocade and vinyl
armchairs angled at the screen,
my brother and me
with an end of the sofa each,
and not a peep from anyone
until the ad break,
when Grandad would put kettle on.

Sunday mornings we'd try integrating
any especially good lines
into our conversations:
*When you've made gravy under gunfire
you can do anything!
Hilda, will you stop that singing! –
It's like a lump of coal
stuck under the back gate!*

Grandad mostly recycled
I'll have hotpot please Betty,
to which Nana invariably replied
you'll have what you're given
and be grateful.

Children celebrate the arrival of the Sabbath

The lighting of the candles
Baroch ata adonai
Before we drink the squash
Elohaynu melech ha'olum
Before we eat the bread
Asher kiddushanu b'mitzvatov
We stand as still as we can
Vetzivanu l'hadlik n'er
Until this prayer is over
Shel shabat
Not long now
Amen

The fruit of the vine
Baroch ata adonai
We pray to the orange squash
Elohaynu melech ha'olum
Neat on brown catering trays
Borei pre ha'gofin
A mouthful in each glass
Amen

The fruit of the earth

Baroch ata adonai
Blessed are the cubes of bread
Elohaynu melech ha'olum
The ones with no crust are the best ones
Hamotze lechem min ha'aretz
We can take three, even four pieces
Amen

Leaflet accompanying his prescription

Talk to your Pharmacist if you
take Beta-blockers or Medicines that make you Drowsy
Talk to your Doctor if you may be Pregnant   If you are Breast-
feeding   If you plan to become   If symptoms do not
If you develop new symptoms   If you are

Do not if you have ever had
Nerve damage   Ringworm   Allergic reactions
Heart failure   Do not with Paracetamol or Anti-
coagulants   Avoid if intolerant   If pump has not been worked
for a short period   re-prime   Never mix with Alcohol

Swallow morning and evening with water
for a week   Do not chew   If Drowsy do not operate
Never take extra if you wake   Do not allow to freeze   Do not
use after   If you ingest by mistake
Skip at least one

You may drink Alcohol
If you accidentally overdose do not worry
Go immediately to Casualty   If you feel no better
Resume as soon as you remember   Apply a thin layer   Wait
one hour   A single Dose may be enough

If you experience Tingling   Flushing
Cramps   Palpitations   Skin rash   Weakness
Bleeding or Swelling of face tongue lips or throat   Drowsiness
Confusion   Increased growth in unexpected places
Make another Appointment

Keep out of reach of Children
Away from naked flame   Ask your Pharmacist
about disposal   Do not in household waste   Set aside
some time each day to Relax and Unwind   Keep this safe
You may need to read it again

The Door

I wonder how my Cypriot grandfather lived
in England for 46 years without central heating.

The door, he would shout whenever I stepped
into his living room, not trusting me to close it

without being told. Cold air trying
to repatriate the room; one electric heater,

our only defence. British-born but heat-loving,
my home has central heating on in every room

at least nine months of the year;
mother and I make a mock-Mediterranean.

I wonder if my grandfather never paid
to heat his whole house because

it was never really home and he knew
the heat would be waiting on his return.

The First of March

fresh foliage is honoured – Ovid, Fasti, Book 3,
trans. Anne and Peter Wiseman

Tall willow wands bought from a shop, their silver buds
like nylon fur, fill stoneware jars. I keep them dry

so they won't drop. Outside, spring stirs, the willows light
with green. Indoors, no moisture sucked through stem

or vein, no catkin flowers appear, no messy pollen sheen,
no stain; no rosy spur of folded tissue comes to leaf:

this year there will be no May Day sheaf, no jilted lover's
wilting sprig around my brave attention-seeking hat,

no coffined bower beneath a swaying wind,
no winter's wreath.

ABCs

Thursday evenings would always creep
in and we knew that meant one thing:
    Ka Kha Ga Gha.

While Mummy buttoned us into smart clothes —
    Ka Kha Ga
                Gha —

shovelled *rotli* and *ringra nu shak* into our mouths —
    Ka Kha
        Ga
              Gha —

piled us into our red Cavalier —
    Ka Kha Ga?
                Gha —

chimed the way —
    Ka Ka
        Kha Kha
          Ga —
   through the — *Ka*
      steel gates — *Kha*
         heaved — *Ga*
            us out — *Gha*
                and we dragged — *Ka*
        our legs — *Kha*
          all the way to our door —

Ka Kha Ga — slipped
   Ga Gha — in
      as Sir settled — *Ka*
        the din — *Kha*
          and began — *Ga*
            to take note:

              — Shruti?
                — *Gha.*
                   — Pardon?
                     — Er... present!
                      I mean, present!

* Ka Kha Ga Gha – The first four letters of the Gujarati alphabet
  rotli – chapati
  ringra nu shak – aubergine curry

19

Tahara

Tahara (heb.): lit. 'purification'; the process of
ritually preparing a body for a Jewish burial.

On the table, carnations.
I hate them. These furled, crimped pinks
my mother would buy.
Even now
she is tightly wound –

the women twist the sheet around her,
over her face,
before letting me into the room;
give me dirt from the Holy Land
to sprinkle into her plywood coffin,

read the Hebrew prayer with me
in their shtetl accent.
I slow them down,
too tired to translate sense
as well as sound.

We lift the lid together, nail it closed.
It's a good deed to care for a body,
to accompany a soul to its grave.
It takes time to learn how to wash
each fold of skin,

how to fold a shroud.
They had studied for this.
They had taken their time.
Longer than promised, than usual.
I'd waited with a friend –

we were meant to recite psalms,
instead we stared
at the linoleum,
could only imagine
what they worked to cleanse.

Everything bad

is happening somewhere else
and not in the park. Trees open their shadows out
like veins on the back of a hand.
A child in lilac leggings does the splits
and collapses, giggling. The sun weaves a thread
through the railings' rounded tops. Youths heap sweatshirts
to mark goals, and on the hill's green plaid
a dog the colour of last year's leaves gyrates.
Everything as I jog has a hand-held camera look –
sticky buds on a branch jerk by
in close-up, and the far river tilts its steel-blue hook.
All vestiges of urban sin are washed away
in the spring light. Here, no-one is wounded or crying
or afraid, or if they are, it's not showing.

Mehndi Night

They said Indian patterns would be best:
the peacocks, the paisleys, of course the girl-boy faces,
and they said his name should be a whisper
in your hand and that the rose-petalled sheets
would wait until he traced it, and they said
you should seal it with lemon and sugar,
and even if it itched and the smell of wet made you sick,
you should sleep with it on, and they said, the next day,
you shouldn't wash as water weakens the stain,
and they said, instead, you heat your hands over a stove,
and the darker the coppered hue,
the deeper his love.

And you on that red stool in the middle of the room,
you said,
'Okay.'

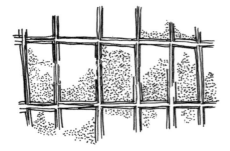

Mending hedges

In Dentdale they're mending hedges while the weather's dry, in time for the frantic grow of May. I'm paying attention, though I don't know the wood that makes the straight poles, the liggers laid like twigs in a witch's besom.

I'd guess it's beech: its thin, fine bark the colour of a seal. Today the big raptors hang above the stacked dykes, the pastures full of lambs still ribby in their skins.

I'm stunned by all the things I'll never know about this world, watching the shepherd strike out up the fellside in the winter boots he's patched with tape. One whistle flings the wiry collie outward in a fast loop to buzz the ewes.

I feel like I spend so much time being frightened, I miss the signs of what's coming again and again. The shepherd and the shirtless men on their knees in the hedge – their thick knives shining on the verge –

will survive. When the wind turns, when the tups lie down against the stones, when the trees leaf later and later than ever, they know what it means.

I drive back into the city bringing nothing with me, carrying nothing I could possibly use.

Liver Bird

I

Saturday night comes caped in glitter
and she's been ready since Wednesday.
She frees each roller strategically, kirby grips

like Jenga blocks securing the structure –
the nest on her crown fit for doves.
The air grows hairspray thick and she could die

happy on a perfumed cloud but instead
phones a Delta, moth-wing lashes guiding her
towards the neon lights of a Seel Street bar.

II

On heel-scuffed basement dance floors
she is illuminated, heart like a ferry
carrying the weight of a people.

The night bends over the Mersey
as if to see itself reflected one last time
before morning. She hobbles barefoot

over Bold Street, sees herself reflected
in a puddle: a merwoman, hair like seaweed,
broken glass like sand between her toes.

The Girl With the Rubber Boot

'Give it some welly girl!'
my dad yells from the sidelines,
making himself laugh at his own pun.

And I try my best, though
welly wanging's not really my forte.

I don't have the shoulders for it –
not broad ones like Mr Brown,
champion three years in a row.

I wang with all my might and watch
the judge with his measuring stick.

A personal best!
My dad cheers until he's hoarse.

Mr Brown does better.
I settle for my second place rosette.

Maypole Dancing in 2000
Wellow, Nottinghamshire

Each year the same, with difference; and this year
rain-weighted clouds fled the first bugle notes.
The old blackbird's singing, said a man who knew
how Wellow weather kicks its heels, and smiles
for circling dancers.
　　　　　　　　So this morning's storms
polished the lustre on red hawthorn, oak,
white lilac archways, and the single plait
of past and present. The last thousand years
tipped over, ours now, catching in their web
the fifty years since dancing here revived.

Now Queens from these past fifty years – and more,
two who danced Barber's Pole and Gypsies Tent
before the War carved more names in the Hall –
stare, honoured, as the new Queen sets the dance
spinning; the red, white, blue, remembering.

Remembering what's clipped for scrapbooks – crowns,
her dress, her gold attendants (girls, who now
watch daughters' daughters weave the double plait) –
how this year's exhibition brought it back.
Was that your dress? Oh yes. *Now, who was that …?*
tracing the names and faces, loved and lost.
Amo, Amas – like yesterday, like then;

until the organ stirs, and spins a dance
fresh as May grass, weaves for delighted eyes
the new Millennium; children who've learned
already how to thread their mothers' ways
with future patterns, and a rhythm sprung
out of this Green, and all the dances passed
on before history thought to write them down.

Loud, long applause; another year is cast
before the Queen, her dancers, and her Crown.

DEREK LITTLEWOOD

Kernowek Stone

Bes den heb tavas a golhas e dir
A man who has lost his tongue has lost his land

Heller stone teasy as an adder: a serpent in your kitchen boy
why you fetch her away? You pulled her from the salt strand,
      took her
upcountry serpentine splash red and black, fetched her from
the zawn at Kynance cove on Lizard. Picked up smooth in hand
chill to the touch; you pour water over to make her colours glow
handsome. Serpentine and schists, gabbro, hornblende, gneiss –
      but you see
it slows grass growth, toxic rock here. Sometime antimony,
      arsenic, gold
remain in the old shafts. Close your eyes, hold her to your ear:
      you hear
the cry of the red beak chough circle the cliff. Chiach-chiaa -chi-ah
tschraah- chough. Touch your lips to her then after you kiss salt
you might sing a sea rhyme:

> *O a stone of herrings is forgot,*
> *a crann, a creel,*
> *a crabber pot,*
> *the pilchards swum,*
> *the bleddy lot,*
> *gone west over the sea.*

Leave off that pusser's rum boy, else you see double.
Stand a trumpet shell in your hot sunny window an years later

a bloody trickle leak across the dust as she pines for the sea
so why do you think this serpent has no feeling, no chough
   tongue?
In her fastness she shall sing the music of the stones this
   lightness.
Dare to sleep with her under your pillow, uneasy between your
   thighs
she might offer you a dream vision, you'd wake stone crazy
channelling Jock Graham, and Peter Lanyon gliding high over
   Lanyon Quoit.
This am a mazy stone, better hoy her back boy, after this long
   stank
a hike over moors downcountry. Heller stone belongs at home.

* A glossary of Cornish and dialect terms:
  Kernowek – Cornish language
  heller – wild natured
  upcountry – out of Cornwall
  teasy – moody
  zawn – ravine
  crann – large measure of herring
  mazy – confused, mad
  hoy – throw (English dialect)
  stank – hike
  men – stone
  sarfven – serpentine

National Lottery

Every four years, sometimes less,
I go to an unfamiliar building:
pub extension, Sunday school room, community hall.

I sneak through the ballot bouncers on the door.
I tell them nothing, face a blank canvas.
Check no one is looking and leave my mark.

I do this in secret.

For just a day the tables are stacked, yoga mats postponed.
Always the same graffiti:
childhood scrawl with jumbo pencil.
Community Art for a day.

My two-stroke signature folded, boxed,
sealed with wax, driven across town;
poured out like paper fish onto collapsible tables.
Sorted into species:
the rotten spoiled ones thrown away.

I await late night numbers
for next day's prize.
Wonder if my name on the ledger underlined
has counted or
counts for nothing.

Discarded, left to flap on the town hall floor.

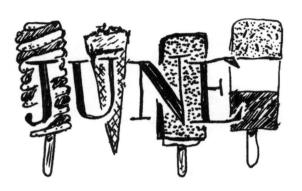

Nettle eating contest

Look at us, wearing red and white, just
look at us, chomping thin spiny bodies
like the medieval stage devils that were really
a poor soul shivering in a deer's head. Will you just
look at us: we are winter
devastating the meadows. The winner
holds up long stalks, devoid of any leaves.

Mrs J

I'm as British as the smell of stale vinegar on the papers that litter the pavement outside the Irish bookies on Kilburn High Road. Mrs J's taking me on a cruise you see, when her horse comes in. Seeing as we had fingerless gloves on the last time she barbecued, I'm hoping that's soon. The weather has to be better than this in the Holy Land.

Mrs J's white teeth are British, under the hat she wears with matching court shoes. She gets knockoffs from the market traders. Mrs J's been the local midwife all their lives. They give her ten percent off and ask after her kids. Mrs J says they are all children of Empire. Then she laughs but I don't get it.

Black British — not like the black in the Union Jack the last time the skins marched. Whatever; I'm not going nowhere. Neither is Mrs J. We're here to stay. We're as British as a prawn cocktail for starters, as poppadoms before vindaloo, saying please and thank you.

At the old people's home when I visit Mrs J still says 'When my horse comes in.' I don't tell her I stopped placing bets years ago when the bookies shut down and it all went electronic. I say 'I know; the weather's better in the Holy Land and are you going to drink that tea.'

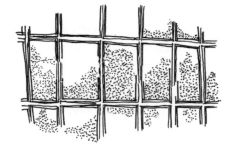

CLAIRE COLLISON

The Support Group

1. *Everybody needs a bosom for a pillow*

We form a horseshoe, handing around the prostheses
like cakes; they warm to our touch.

We learn the life of a bra is the same
as that of a pillow (six months).

Passing on a lace one called *Caress*,
I tell the group, I miss

my satin balcony; I gave it to my niece.

2. *Stockholm Syndrome*

We miss the theatre of the blue curtain;
you taking our temperature
and weighing us each three weeks.

We miss the drinks machine,
and how everything was wipe-clean.

We miss the botanical photographs,
and reclining in peach Lazeeboys.

We miss you asking after our bowels,
and for any unaccountable bruising.

We miss packing little lunches; the litany
of drugs, double-checked, with our names on.

3. *Novena*

Saint Agatha, who rolled in broken crockery,
intercede for my tribe, the one no one elected to join.

My new friend calls us the One Tit Club,
although to the untrained eye
we are unremarkable.

We swelter under wigs, wafting the air
with our pocket fans.

Saint Agatha, who is bowling-green flat,
we too are unnatural as golf courses:
give us our collective noun.

Saint Agatha, who stems fire, and halts
volcanoes and other eruptions,
pray for us, you freak.

Midsummer 2017

A town planner slept and as he slept
  he dreamt that every high street
    in the country aligned along a grid.
      Village, suburb, city – all laid
        east to west, so seen from above via
          Google Earth or Charles Booth
            all were perfectly barcode or pinstripe.
              Once a year, late in June, he had the sun
                set plumb between the buildings at the top
                  of all of them, slotting in the gap
                    between Boots and Next, New Look
                      and Primark, or Costa and the Heart
                        Foundation shop. As clean as a potted red: he
                          watched it drop. Or not. He woke the night
                            that in the market towns, something snaps.
                        Up north, every bronze minister
                      gets his dignity offset with a hi-vis
                    orange wizard's hat; down south,
                  the shopping centre fountains foam
                with Fairy Liquid. Neptune may thrust
              his barbecue utensil to the sky
            but a trillion bubbles surge the lip
          of his marble bowl. Feathered
        with suds, italic with shots, lads,
      singing, grapple in the lather, singing,
    arms round each other, singing,
  mate, now that's a fucking anthem!

KIM M. RUSSELL

Seaside Beauties

On a chilly, wet July afternoon,
attendants are unfolding a platoon
of stripy deckchairs on the pier.

Under sagging sunshades or in see-through
plastic macs, holidaymakers stare
at a bevy of beauties in bathing suits
with carefully coiffured hair,
counting goose-bumps on mottled skin.

The compere and resident comedian
bounds onto the stage with a grin,
clears his throat, taps the microphone,
and the beauty contest begins.

Teetering on high-heeled, sling-back shoes,
fluttering false eyelashes against the drizzle,
teenage girls face cheers and catcalls
as mascara runs and tempers sizzle.

To an impressionable child of six or seven,
unaware of nineteen-sixties feminism,
such a glamorous parade was heaven

and an unattainable ambition
for a skinny, bespectacled girl
with sandy hair and not a single curl.

Showtime

Two carrots on a white plate.
Two turnips (tied). Longest bean.
Three tomatoes on a white plate.
Five tomatoes attached to stem.
Five leeks, cleaned, roots intact.
One or more vegetables not previously
mentioned. Foetid mud, pork fat,
pulled pork in pallid buns.
Carved sticks with ewes-horn handles,
shooting socks. Clay guns,
wet wool feet. Pimm's in plastic glasses.
Young farmers (female) toss heady manes
at young farmers (male, stolid). Both lust.

An edible face. Musical tyres and lady stealing.
Limerick starting *there was an old lady*
from London. Lakeland terriers, dog, bitch
and puppy. First birthday card
for Princess Charlotte, hand-drawn.
Five penned ewes with Roman noses.
Texel-snouted wether hoggs, Texel
dry-aged lamb. Gimmers on the hoof.
Farmers (male). Farmers' (wives).
Victoria sponge of good texture, displayed
on a family plate. Envelope addressed
to The Queen. Beer in pungent mud.

Vintage tractors circle the show field,
maximum four miles an hour.
Grand Parade stock led by steel
nose rings. Threshing machines
winnow sticks, harvest waves.
Small boys perch on ancient
knees, some small girls. Circling.
Champion tup bagged with promise,
a tudor cow, wearing gloss, trends
a chair hide. Percheron plaited horses.
A fearsome bull trades fertile juices
for ancestral freedoms. Scares the shit.
Champion of Champions breeds the future.

Swan–Upping

Swans gliding like a melody
on rippling semiquavers; skiffs
row up to meet them, beating time –
dip and pull, dip and pull.

'All up!' The courtly dance begins:
birds centre, boats around the edge.
And five, six, seven, eight
lift and tie, weigh and mark, release.

Swans and cygnets, ringed and claimed,
take their mute parade downstream.
The men pick up the beat again –
dip and pull, dip and pull.

Paintbox colours on the Thames:
scarlet, white and royal blue.
At Romney Lock they stand and toast
Her Majesty, Seigneur of Swans.

One wears a feather in his cap.

On July 28th

the dining table was dragged out to the lawn
and its mottled surface polished to chestnut.
It was covered with the spider web of lace
crocheted long before we were born
and used only for this homecoming.

Red lemonade, sweet with a hint of spice:
each bottle a different coloured straw
stood like guardsmen at each place
set with fine china. A complete set
waited for our summer playmates.

She had taken the trouble to make red jelly
in glass moulds, stored in the recesses
of the cupboard, to unmould them
so that their fragile domes shuddered
with anticipation of ice cream.

When we children had wandered off,
soaked with sugar and adult chat,
they would take our places for tea
that would last for hours. Friends
would come and go. Neighbours
walking the road would call over the wall:
'You're home for the holidays?'

AUGUST

PAM THOMPSON

Carnival, Leicester

In March, Leonie stitches her costume –
peacock feathers onto a wire hoop, white ones
on a tiger-print headband, fans them into a plume,

fans them, blitzes glue from a gun.
In April she glues rhinestones from Amazon
to her pink bikini, huge crystal tears, tries it all on,

sends photos to her family in Antigua.
In May, her auntie visits. She was queen
when she was younger, has photos too, a phoenix

dressed in gold flanked by sphinxes. *Emancipation* –
she tells her wondering niece – *what it's about,
don't forget*. And she doesn't – in June

when it rains on her dancers' rehearsal, in hot
July when she writes up her PhD – it blazes
fiercest in August when they're lined up

at Vicky Park gates, all shimmer and shimmy – it sways
as she sways and the steel drums hammer out
its rhythm and it pulses in her blood for days.

In March Leonie stitches her costume –
sticks feathers on a headdress, fans them into a plume.

Torchlight Procession, Sidmouth
5th August 2016

Giles Fraser believes that faith, fundamentally, begins from the community.

Here is England splayed on the Esplanade,
out-candling the Channel's mantlepiece.

Others say that faith is an intensely personal thing and object to organised religion. I don't know whether you can be intensely inward and I wouldn't like to try. And besides, the statement is self-evidently false.

The men move forward in four-four-and-a-half
with bells mounted by leather to their feet.

Giles Fraser stopped believing in God at the funeral of a baby. There were few mourners and the mother had carved the baby's name into her arm. Giles Fraser put his belief, instead, into the church, the congregation, their collective understanding, collective will, stored it like a back-up file and, slowly, among them, he found his faith again.

Thom Gifford waves his torch and shambles to
Old Tom of Oxford and The Postman's Knock.

I think you feel it in a theatre (when the play is really good). It gives the stage its power, that collective will, that synaptic sense that runs from skull to skull around the room.

The Lantern-making Workshop files through
to where the people of five towns have flocked.

I felt in the air that night: faith, between the stomp of the morris women's clogs and the skip of the Obbie Orse and the clacking of the clackers and the glowing of the glowsticks and the sense of England curling its lip and lapping its tail and the putting out of torches in the sea.

Arise Great Western! Fool's Gambit arise!
Arise John Gasson! Arise Grand Union!

Some people say faith is like the team-building game where you fall back with your eyes closed and another person catches you but faith is neither as physical nor as exclusive. Faith is a troupe of morris dancers sequenced along a seafront. Faith is a room of fully-grown adults pretending to be spitfires. Faith is a line of torches, aflame, windblown, withstanding. Faith is a street when the street is full of people who have chosen to be on that street.

With every colour ribbon, every size
of pipe, bodhran, accordion and drum,
we'll sweep the old year back into July
and sing O Kafoozalum, Kafoozalum.

Break

Two men are sharing a fag break
on the outside stairs of a multi-storey
portakabin. White office shirts, no tie,
dark trousers, brown hair, indeterminate
age and waistlines. They don't seem
to be talking, just looking outwards
together, their only view
wrong-side-of-tracks light industry
and full summer trees. Stood in the middle
of a dull day, middle floor of the block
painted greyish green, both oblivious
to the stalled train. At least they have
something they're breaking from.
When the train moves, we leave them there.

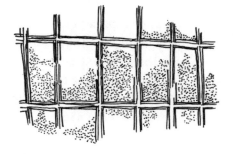

An Ordinary Miracle

Breezy evening on Porthcressa:
a small crowd has gathered,
gazing at the shrine
where steam wafts like incense.
The van rocks gently
as Eugene, light on his feet
as any ballroom dancer,
turns between fryer and counter,
blue eyes scanning the orders.
Grasping a fish by the tail,
he dips it into the batter,
dropping it into the oil
in a single fluid gesture.
Two deft shakes of the scoop
and chips fan out crisply
into neatly ranged boxes.
Three patient acolytes
each have a part in the ritual,
until, at last, one of them
calls out my name
and delivers a blessing
with the salt and vinegar.

Walnuts in August

everyone tells the same small
stories of you   *twenty-five*
        this time
          every year   those old
          walnuts   split the room again

Half of us   can laugh
at how you ate grass
        doing the caterpillar in the garden, or
         saying *shite* to nana when you really didn't
mean to blend   *shine* and *light* together.
Such a Good

Nice Boy.
        boys now, get blown to heaven like
        those old Action Men we used to
                  slide

            down

      strings

from the top
window to

the small
  fern
   tree   with those
        ready curved-fingered hands; ready

for holding guns for
          punching back
                    for
                         sliding
                                   to
                                        an old
                                             fern
                                             branch

from the top
window.   The other half of us

can't. We cannot stop crying
and we cannot start laughing
          when they mention your name
          with walnuts and no (your-)laugh
          to wash the lovely down   and make it
                                             stay.

pastoral

big garden   green sea   wendy-house-ship   or   spy-
base-roof to neighbours' living room • brush oars and brooms
and rake paddles   air spades   loo-roll telescopes
old table wreckage • shell-suit   pirates!   stick swords
stick spears   stick bows   stick arrows   stick sticks
bin-lid shields   pear bombs and pear grenades • french soup
witches brew; worms and slugs and rain and snails and 'stuff' n'
'nufin'! magnifying fire maker • bum bag treasure keeper
survival   'five more minutes' pleas and 'it's.NOT.fair!'s •
Lucky Charms Frosties   Apple Jacks and Rainbow Brite
Pop Tarts! Rola Cola   Wagon Wheels x3 (on sale)   P i n k
Wafers and Smiley Faces   Alphabet Fries and homemade
chips paper cones   fish-shaped-fish   and   Bubbaloos!
cornflake pie and jam sandwich squares squashed just 'right'
chocolate cake on mint custard plates Sprinkles   and   Angel
Delight Fun Dips   Nerds and Candy 'Cigs'   S p a c e
Ships   Vimto; 'hot or cold?' • fruit-scented pens and canvas-
walls   Casio Keyboard and Rubics Cube   Viewmaster! •
roller skates • Chatter-Box telephone •   living   room;   shop\
hospital\ battle field; playing-card-cities and blu-tack bombs
and missile deals • pulling teeth out   stringed   to   prams?
:/   ballerina in a box and Glow Worm   Cabbage Patch
Care Bears   Cindy and Stretch - - - Armstrong; the secret
syrup stash. Adam's tags   Ethel Austin's and No Frills sale bits
and Gap   Netto • roller blades and Kickers and 'I don't

want to wear them anymore!'s • Sharp combi-telly; channels One to Four • videos • M.J. Productions by Siblings&Co. • *Magic Roundabout   Teenage Mutant Ninja Turtles! Power Rangers! He-Man   Rainbow   Raggedy Anne and Andy* • Blockbuster videos • *E.T   The Labyrinth* and *Terminator* Two (not Three) and 'itt's *Thriiillerrr*'   and   'Annie   Are You Okay' and anybody's clothes   *Honey I Blew Up The Kids!*   Sega Mega Drive   Master System   *Alex the Kid Super Mario   Sonic   PacMan   Crash   Bandicoot* and *Street Fighter* • cassettes!   radio recordings   brush microphones   Sony Walkman   ® • mini mattress; sleigh! mountains made of stairs! shrieks and yells and 'too much noise it's bloody laaate!'s •   bedtime milk. *Heartbeat*   on Sunday 'b4 skool' means   time to sleep   b u b b l i n g under quilts   '*Heartbeat* – why does a love kiss stay in myy memory'   suppressing laugh and squeal • couch   h o t water bottles on the side; the seal // Resistance… channel Five.

all this, anytime we all get home for eid.

SEPTEMBER

Conkers

Grip it tight
pull it back
hit them hard
hear them CRACK!

The Last Katlama

It always tastes of those aching memories:
when hands no paler than flaking pastry
roll rows of balls from dough and minced meat,
spice soaking into us like brown-red *mendhi*;

when we are hot oil, laughter bubbling,
Bollywood, Bon Jovi, Whitney and Mohammed Rafi.
All my sisters are *Khabie Gham Khabi Khushi*
and want to dance around the kitchen with somebody.

This is my father's recipe:
flour and water and clear yellow *kyoh*
folded in on itself and then folded more;
tonight touching tomorrow morning –
the moon fat in the middle, a *pera* ready for filling.

We are a well-oiled production line,
counting *katlame*, cardboard boxes and minutes to midnight.
Drop this moment, flattened; watch it fry,
first sink then swell with all we kneaded into it and rise.

Tomorrow we feed your arguing brothers;
my cousins who are always insulting each other;
the niece you find irritating, the nephew who moans
and your son who on all other days eats alone –

our arms tender from the squeezing and the pulling
and in the palm of our hands somehow still holding
this perfect round proof of love
and what it means to share it.

* katlama – flat round meat-filled Pakistani pastry
  kyoh – ghee
  pera – ball of dough

The Abbots Bromley Horn Dance

How the reindeer antlers ended up here,
in this Staffordshire hamlet, isn't recorded.
They've been carbon-dated all the way back
to the early years of the last millennium,
though when the dance started is anyone's guess.
Some experts dismiss it – *A Victorian*
invention… corrupt, jack-pudding nonsense –
but a Royalist general claimed he saw it
when he was a boy, before the Commonwealth
banned such things. Whatever: come Wakes Monday
they're here, members of two local families,
Fowells and Bentleys – six men carrying
the horns; the motleyed fool with a bouncer's
buzz-cut, a pig's bladder wobbling on a stick;
the old guy soothing his red melodeon;
the hobby-horse man, who yanks a string
to clack the gee-gee's jaw; Maid Marian
(a bloke in drag), ignoring the giggling kids.

Tourist, blow-in, don't ask what it means.
All we can say is this: today the rasp
of trucks and four-by-fours is brought to a halt;
the village reclaims its streets, with ice-cream cones
or pints in hand, to watch the men go through.
Irony can't taint their measured jig;

they carry something none of us can touch.
The dance resists all questioning. Its restless
impulse drives it on, like sweeping autumn
rain, that comes each year, again, again.

Hi-Vis and the Whorl

We'd given up on there ever being a bus
when the woman with purple nails told us
the next was due.

The driver was being trained: Hi-Vis sprawled
along the sideways seat, shouting instructions –
Overtake, he ordered the driver, about to pull in at a stop.

As we slowed at a junction, a young man
reached the door, pleading to be let on –
Ignore it, said Hi-Vis; the driver pulled away.

The young man ran over dual carriageways, through traffic.

We all watched: the purple-nailed woman, the woman
taking her kids to school, the man who could have used his pass
if the bus had been four minutes later.

The young man ran.
He wore a striped cotton scarf, and a jacket:
it was impossible to tell if he was mad.

The bus reached the stop; the young man reached it, too.

You didn't stop, he said. There were three of us. You didn't stop.
There was another bus in front, Hi-Vis replied; he didn't have to stop.
It wasn't going to Broadway, said the young man. He took off his scarf.

He was handsome, his hair well cut. He wasn't mad.
Every one of us on the bus was relieved:
he'd made it and he wasn't mad.

We can't know where the other bus is going, said Hi-Vis –
    and he knew
we all knew that wasn't right or even true. I've got an
    interview,
Young Man said, paying his fare to the driver; you freaked
    me out.

We wanted to give up our seats and offer him water; to
    tell him:
you were right, Hi-Vis was wrong.
We are sorry for the way the bus didn't stop.
We are sorry you had to run.
It is lucky you are so fit (look: you are hardly sweating!
Your crisp striped shirt is hardly damp!)

I sat behind the whorl in his nice hair –
it must have been cut the day before.
I wondered what kind of a job he was going for.

I wanted to give him a note
to give to the interviewer,
to explain the extenuating circumstances.

But he didn't need a note.
He would be fine.
We could all see that.

We got off at the same stop, outside Primark.
I turned to him and smiled.
He smiled back – a bright, open smile, like he'd
    already got the job.

Good luck, I said, unnecessarily.

RAMONA HERDMAN

Blackberrying

Blooded young, we waded
into the hooked shallows of hedges,
caught up and cut in our toddler blundering, dirty
with gritty juice and dotted-line scratches.

We without-ritual British, we atheists.
Hippies' children, grown up
in the world they believe they changed –
we have blackberrying as our sacrament.

At school, neater children wouldn't eat the berries,
said their mothers said no, said
they had worms in that would eat our insides
and poke out of our bumholes.

Now we go every year, like it's Midnight Mass.
We avoid the dog zone at the bottom of the bushes.
Tell each other that by Michaelmas
the Devil will have pissed them bitter.

We take offal-heavy carrier bags of berries
to our parents, too old now for all that bother.
We pick the children out of the tangled footings.
We cook pies and crumbles in our own kitchens,
competently. We placate the gods.

Edge Hill

'All day it has rained…'

Those sullen words at war with boredom
are true again out here, walking the ridge
that stands between two midland counties.

From a bench seat the panorama spreads:
John Leyland's 'champion land' of Feldon
still demands its gage of solid husbandry.

As the tractor ploughs an uphill furrow
its straining engine growls across the rain,
grows softer easing the downhill stretch.

He sits there and lets the land take him,
an English Sisyphus in oilskin and cap
working the farm below a Saxon boundary.

Up here, our conversation is the gossip
of raindrops on leaves and the squelch
of drenched soil – until mid-afternoon.

Three jets cross the vale in a moment
but leave their low-flying roar behind
to drown the noise of rain and everything.

The tractor's grind is first to emerge
lumbering into the turn, dragging a train
of gulls to the top of the darkening field.

Below us the site of the battle is marked
by the perimeter fence of an arms dump,
the fields full of barrows full of bombs.

21st October
An apology to Cox and Russet

The air thins. I stand underneath the trees,
contrite, my hand held up to cup and test
with reverential twist your readiness
to drop onto my waiting palm. And yes,
all this forgetful summer passed away
I've dallied with the long-haul charlatans,
swallowed their false promise shamefully,
their brief sweetness ashes on my tongue.

Blame my impatience, my green eagerness
for your so complicated English hit, vinaceous
under Pippin's ruddy flush or sweet nut
dressed in chafed-cheek rusticoat.

The day's edge narrows into true autumn.
You hang, a gathering of light. Is it time?

NoVEMBER

Mischief Night

Miggy Night was the big one round our way,
bigger than Guy Fawkes or Hallowe'en.
The shops ran out of glue and garden twine,
old ladies hid their dustbin lids away,

neighbours with any sense locked up their cats,
some took tubs in, others removed their gates
but nothing stopped us, me and Joan and Kate,
we had our mams' permission to stay out

till late that one night of the year, larking,
carrying out devilment down the lane
armed only with Uhu and balls of string
and afterwards, unnoticed, crept back in,

innocents no more. The deed was done
and no-one ever asked us where we'd been.

November 5th

Boot-to-boot in mud we've trudged to treachery,
in a dark that seems all the thicker
for the near light of the bonfire, we watch
the sparks flow off in shining rivers, up, up,
and out into black. It seems like hours
we stand there, shuffling the cold from foot to foot,
the tiny stars of our sparklers spitting
from wool-muffled hands. But then the bangs begin.
And the colours. And our ring of shining faces
make a fence around this bright new world,
where bobble hats are softly, briefly dazzled,
and walls for miles rebound with noise.
Those rainbows climbing the wet sky,
like trout swimming up to lip at the skin
between us and everything else.
The silent metal flowers that lift away
like gold leaf flaked by a fingernail.
The sky fills our upturned faces
with colour, fills until our brightness runs over.
Tonight, we are not strangers
to each other.

ANGELA KIRBY

Fall Guy

Traitor, Turnip-head –
that stopped your smirking
even though, ever merciful
to the undeserving,
before we lit the bonfire,
I'd strangled you with a tie.
Still, seeing you burn
upset the children
and, far worse –
will I never learn –
when you'd gone, when all
your sticks were charcoal
and we were dancing
round your pyre,
I wanted you back,
to see you rise
from that pall of ashes,
black-faced, soot-eyed,
trailing red-hot cinders,
wanted you, smouldering
here in my cold bed
and up to your old tricks.

Saturday Soup

Bevan is smiling into his soup, juggling with
the choice of dumpling or dasheen to devour.
Do you think things will ever get better for us?
I'm hugging the bowl my mother places before me;
the smell draws me in. The swirling, twirling
wisp of heat that snakes into the air hypnotizes me.
He breaks the trance and continues, *I'm sick and tired*
of all of this – pointing to the colour of his skin –
I'm tired of fighting and fitting in.
I'm sucking on a bone and find a response
amongst the sweet potatoes and cho-cho.
War is not the answer, only love can conquer hate.
He laughs; we chew on other thoughts
and let Marvin Gaye tell us *What's going on.*

I was writing city lyrics,
the poetics of the oppressed;
Bevan was an Urban Rembrandt
drawing revolutions of the young.
He was six-feet wound-up length of muscle –
oftentimes we'd wrestle and play –
fight until bruises mushroomed, leaving
fallouts that blew away friendship
for that split second, barely standing
until rescued by the bonds of laughter.

We were brothers not by blood, but by the
late evenings where we sat in front of electric fires,
told stories to the dawn of the new morning
and wore out the tape of *Enter the Dragon*.

Frank

I never knew my father's father, Frank.
He died before I was born. He drove a tank
In the war, and drank himself to death when he
Came back. Took thirty years. I'll never be
A man in that mould – hard-worn, hard-won and all
The rest – and that's for the best; it wouldn't suit
My constitution. Too much alcohol
And I get maudlin. 'Mine's a pint of stout.'
My father asked him once why he'd never become
A vicar, as he'd planned, and he replied
That in the desert, from time to time you'd run
Into a complication, where you'd find
The tank got stuck, with something lodged in its tracks.
Get down and run to pull it out and it
Would be a limb. An arm or leg drawn back
Into the mechanism. 'So you'd have to get
The bugger out before you could go on.
Then on you'd go. And so, before too long,
I didn't want the things I'd thought I might.
Dead friends' limbs in tank tracks… Another pint?'

JERROLD BOWAM

Let's all go down the pub

A living room away from home
to meet with friends or sit alone,
have several drinks or nurse just one:
let's all go down the pub.

Behind the bar, find decks of cards
or dominoes; shoot pool, throw darts,
play skittles and bar billiards:
there's all sports at the pub.

Those seeking solace, love or fun;
a stag and hen to be stitched up,
young couples and the local drunk:
there's all sorts at the pub.

Weddings, christenings, Christmas parties,
wakes, gigs, quizzes, karaoke;
you don't want them at your house, so
we do it down the pub.

With wooden beams and polished floors,
long lines of brass taps standing tall,
all kinds of crap hung on the walls:
Ye Olde Great British pub.

In your hotel you're feeling trapped
so you head down to watch the match

and get involved with all the chat:
for now, your local pub.

They're silent as you buy a round
and stare at you till you've sat down
then they'll turn slowly back around:
it's not your local pub.

The Royal Oak, The Rose and Crown,
The Prince of Wales, The Fox and Hounds,
The Bird In Hand, The Ship, The Plough:
a crawl from pub to pub.

A perfect spot to celebrate,
to console and commiserate,
to just meet up with all your mates,
or sit alone and contemplate,

a great place for your next first date,
if early grab a pint and wait,
I'd best stop there or I'll be late,
I'm going down the pub.

December 8th, 1943

On the feast of the Immaculate conception
we wear white satin maternity smocks,
honeycombed in green and yellow,
the school colours, draped
over our gym tunics and silk sashes.
Immaculata, Immaculata, ora pro no-o-bis,
we chant, our voices reedy, unknowing,
through a cloud of breath and incense,
the procession buckling between shadows
and the elbowing trees. Holding candles,
we slip on the narrow path, skating
on thin ice which splinters under us
as the Italian prisoners watch.

Hooded like monks by frost-rimed sacks,
their chilblained hands are telling beads
but their eyes have other tales to tell
and Mother Bracegirdle nips us on
at a sharp pace, rounding up stragglers,
we who look back, precocious
under our white veils. *Immaculata,*
she sings firmly. The banners waver
and recover, the crocodile quickens
towards supper, the feast-day eggs,
real butter on the toast, lace cloths
and yellow stars of winter jasmine
in rinsed-out shrimp-paste jars.

Later, in a blacked-out dormitory,
arms crossed neatly above cold sheets,
in decent preparation for sleep or death,
examining my conscience
from a list of sins thoughtfully provided,
I think of the prisoners – oh their eyes,
their eyes – and notch up, triumphant,
my first Impure Thought.

Tradition

My mother unpicked Christmas. It took years.
She started by stopping her cards, her protest
lost in the drifts of everyone else's
once-a-year warmest wishes. So she dared more –
banned sherry, booed the Queen, fed us
microwaved biryani. One year
she saw it through in bed, the long TV quease,
received us like an ailing empress
(on condition no one brought tinsel, wore red).

Now, she'll spend the day in the quiet
of a Quaker gathering, where the rule
is respect for everyone's unbeliefs.
Or sometimes in the noise of her cabal
of anti-capitalist revolutionaries.
Come the year's dark, they send each other rebel cards –
her favourite that back-arched kitten, arc of hiss,
captioned in scarlet capitals: RESIST!

She has found her fellow cuckoos
and they nest thick as a rookery.
If you could get her to say, she'd say she was free.

The Queens Head at Christmas

Do you remember garnishing the makeshift table with metallic
 coloured crackers,
napkins that you taught me to tenderize into origami fans,
cinnamon candles you let me flambé like Christmas was for me?
Do you remember how Christmas was your only day off through
 the season,
and how you would buckle the pub doors, whip windows closed,
make a Tetris shape of beer-drizzled tables for us to sit, salted
 with stools?
Do you remember how you roasted Hastings' prize-winning
 turkey that year,
held it with padded hands, grease budding at your brow, your
 year's prize,
silver dishes with potato mountains, sprout fountains and
 carrots ladled on my plate?
Do you remember dressing, drizzling the Christmas tree with
 oyster coloured baubles,
plucking the chocolate umbrellas hanging off the pine needles
 like a bird,
sifting presents for me through juggling hands of rainbow
 wrapping paper?
Do you remember we watched outside tinted windows as
 snowflakes peppered the windowsills,
and the roads were iced like the top of your fruitcake?

Do you remember the day was marinated with mulled wine in
    hand-painted mugs,
homemade eggnog steaming in cloudy jugs, then brandies and
    red label vodkas as the evening drew in?
Do you remember the open fire that had danced behind us all
    day, crackling, breathing,
as the final orange embers faded and the day melted into the night?
I wish you could.

Boxing Day Mummer's Play

We're in the car park watching King George and the Turkish Knight ding seven bells out of sheet metal swords: a playground fight over who gets to lie in a puddle. King George is blowing hard but the Knight'll need more than luck to pierce that plastron of blubber.

He's down! He's down! Did you see that? Same as last year, a feint to the left, and the Turk stabs him through the heart. To be honest I was hoping for a bit more blood. It's damp as a cellar and he'll take ages to bleed out.

One by one the mourners appear: Beelzebub, Jack Finney, Father Christmas, and a doctor coming off shift, tired and pissed. There's an ambulance and a resurrection. After that, I lose the plot and we all have a sing song.

First-footing

On New Year's Eve
dark-haired men cross
the threshold bearing
bread, coal, luck.

We would stand small
at the door, quivering.
Knock Knock –
Daddy, freckled with soot,
hands me a lump of coal,
has me on that it's a dusty beetle
or a quarter of powdering onyx,
his hair ashen under the light.

You, Mum, would fetch the bread,
break off corners for us to nibble
before the luck-bearer black-printed our slice
on his journey, leaving the back door ajar –
coming in again through the front.

The two of you wouldn't list the luck
this custom brought us
for fear 'knocking on wood'
didn't work on MDF.

JOAN LENNON

Hogmanay in the Hills

We spill out into the night
to take the mud track back
behind Home Farm,
angle uphill to the ruins
beyond the lochan,
wedge fireworks, precarious
in the stone stumps of wall
and light them

> Summer Fountain
> Dragon's Egg
> Shanghai Surprise

letting loose their stored roar and shriek,
while wind that smells of snow
feathers the sparks sideways

> gold, red, green, silver,
> white so insistent it leaves
> brief black tracks in its wake

as from behind the surrounding shrug of hills,
other year-end-night displays
throw wide white flashes up
to lick the bellies of the clouds.

And in the silence after,
owls call from the woods,
the river makes its sound
like traffic muffled in the dark,
and Schiehallion's broad bulk waits
to be backlit by dawn.

ACKNOWLEDGEMENTS

'Leaflet accompanying his prescription', by Clare Best, was first published in *The Rialto* (84, Autumn 2015).

'First-footing', by Jo Brandon, was first published in her collection *The Learned Goose* (Valley Press, 2015).

'The Abbots Bromley Horn Dance', by Derek Littlewood, was highly commended in the 2011 Larkin and East Riding Poetry Competition, and appeared on their website.

'Edge Hill', by Oliver Comins, was first published in *Poetry Nottingham* in 1988 and, later, in his collection *Oak Fish Island* (Templar Poetry, 2018).

'Tahara', by Aviva Dautsch, was first published in *The North* (50, 2013).

'Blackberrying', by Ramona Herdman, was first published in *The North* in 2017.

'Tradition', by Ramona Herdman, was first published in *The North* in 2014.

'Fall Guy', by Angela Kirby, was first published in *Magma* in 2005, and then in her collection *Dirty Work* (Shoestring Press, 2008).

'December 8th. 1943', by Angela Kirby, was first published in her collection *Mr Irresistible* (Shoestring Press, 2005).

'Everything bad', by Fiona Moore, was first published in *South Bank Poetry* in 2009.

'On July 28th', by Carolyn O'Connell, was previously published in her pamphlet *Between Bamboo* (Hub Editions, 2002) as well as in *Envoi Magazine*.

'Maypole Dancing in 2000: Wellow, Nottinghamshire', by D A Prince was previously published in Newark and Sherwood's *Millennium Chronicle* in 2000.

'Carnival, Leicester', by Pam Thompson, was first published in her collection *Strange Fashion* (Pindrop Press, 2017).

'An Ordinary Miracle', by Louise Walker, was first published in her pamphlet *An Ordinary Miracle* (Barafundle Press, 2017).

ABOUT THE EDITORS

Emma Dai'an Wright is a British-Chinese-Vietnamese publisher, designer and illustrator based in Birmingham, UK. She studied Classics at Brasenose College, Oxford, and worked in ebook production at Orion Publishing Group before leaving in 2012 to set up the Emma Press with the support of the Prince's Trust.

Richard O'Brien is a poet, translator and academic based in Birmingham, UK. He has a PhD on Shakespeare and the development of verse drama. Richard's pamphlets include *The Emmores* (Emma Press, 2014) and *A Bloody Mess* (Valley Press, 2015). His work has featured in *Oxford Poetry, Poetry London* and *The Salt Book of Younger Poets*. In 2017, he won an Eric Gregory Award from the Society of Authors for his poetry.

ABOUT THE AUTHORS

Claire Askew's poetry collection *This changes things* (Bloodaxe, 2016) was shortlisted for an Edwin Morgan Poetry Award, the 2016 Saltire First Book Award, and the 2017 Seamus Heaney Centre and Michael Murphy Memorial prizes. @onenightstanzas.

Dean Atta's debut poetry collection, *I Am Nobody's Nigger*, was shortlisted for the Polari First Book Prize. His poems deal with themes of race, gender, identity and growing up, and have appeared on BBC One's The One Show and several times on BBC Radio 4, BBC World Service and Channel 4.

Casey Bailey is a secondary school senior leader, poet, spoken word performer, author and rapper from Birmingham. His first short collection, *Waiting at Bloomsbury Park*, was published in 2017 by Big White Shed. His first full poetry collection, *Adjusted*, was published in 2018 by Verve Poetry Press.

Sarah Barr lives in Dorset and writes poetry and fiction. Her poems have appeared in *The Frogmore Papers, The Interpreter's House, South*, the *Bridport Prize Anthologies* 2010 and 2016 and

The Templar Anthology 2016. She teaches creative writing in Dorset and for the Open University.

Clare Best's *Excisions*, her first full collection, was shortlisted for the Seamus Heaney Centre Prize, 2012. Other poetry publications include *Treasure Ground, Breastless, CELL, Springlines*. Her latest book is a prose memoir, *The Missing List* (Linen Press, 2018). clarebest.co.uk

Julia Bird grew up in Gloucestershire and now lives in London where she works as a literature promoter. She has published two collections with Salt Publishing (*Hannah and the Monk*, 2008, and *Twenty-four Seven Blossom*, 2013) and an illustrated pamphlet – *Now You Can Look* – with the Emma Press in 2017.

Jerrold Bowam: a British/Canadian writer who aspires to find others who are as amused as his muse, have a predilection for repetition and a penchant for recurrence.

Jo Brandon was born in 1986 and currently lives in West Yorkshire. Jo has a pamphlet, *Phobia* (2012), and a full-length collection, *The Learned Goose* (2015), both with Valley Press. Jo's work has featured in various publications including *The Poetry Review, The North, Butcher's Dog* and *Magma*. www.jobrandon.com

Carole Bromley lives in York where she is the stanza rep and runs poetry surgeries for the Poetry Society. Winner of a number of first prizes, Carole has three collections with smith|doorstop: *A Guided Tour of the Ice House, The Stonegate Devil* and *Blast Off!*, a children's collection.

Alan Buckley is from Merseyside, and now lives in Oxford. He has two poetry pamphlets: *Shiver* (tall-lighthouse, 2009), and *The Long Haul* (HappenStance, 2016). He was highly commended in the 2017 Forward Prizes. He is a poetry editor at ignitionpress, and a school writer-in-residence with the charity First Story.

Shruti Chauhan is a poet and performer from Leicester. In 2018, she won the National Poetry Library's Instapoetry competition and was voted Best Spoken Word Performer at the Saboteur Awards. Shruti's debut pamphlet, *That Which Can Be Heard*, is forthcoming with Burning Eye Books in November 2018.

Claire Collison's publishing credits include *Butcher's Dog, The Compass, Island Review, Bare Fiction, Elbow Room*, and *Templar Anthology*. Artist-in-residence at the Women's Art Library, Claire is currently touring her single-breasted life modelling monologue, 'Truth is Beauty'. writingbloomsbury.wordpress.com

Oliver Comins lives in West London and writes poems about people, sport, landscape and growing up. He grew up in Warwickshire, the county where Edge Hill is located. Templar Poetry has published three of his pamphlets since 2014 and a full length collection, *Oak Fish Island*, in 2018.

Aviva Dautch has an MA in creative writing from Goldsmiths and a PhD in poetry from Royal Holloway. Her poems are published in magazines including *Agenda, Modern Poetry in Translation* and *The Poetry Review*. In 2017 she won the Poetry School/Nine Arches Press Primers Prize for emerging voices.

Tracy Davidson lives in Warwickshire and writes poetry and flash fiction. Her work has appeared in various publications and anthologies, including: *Mslexia, Modern Haiku, Shooter, Journey to Crone, Ekphrastia Gone Wild, The Emma Press Anthology of Aunts* and *In Protest: 150 Poems for Human Rights*.

Ian Dudley's most recent publications have been in *Ink, Sweat and Tears, The Rialto* and *Zoomorphic*. He has won the Oxonian Review (2015) and Aesthetica (2017) poetry competitions, and featured in Eyewear's *The Best New British And Irish Poets 2016*.

Clementine Ewokolo-Burnley is a migrant writer, mother and community worker. She has been a finalist in the Bristol Short Story Prize Competition 2017, the Miles Morland Scholarship Award and received an Honourable Mention in the Berlin Writing Prize Competition. @decolonialheart

Steve Harrison born in Yorkshire and now lives in Shropshire. His work has appeared in Emergency Poet collections, Wenlock Festival, *The Physic Garden, Pop Shot, Mid-Winter Solstice, The Curlew* and *Poets' Republic*. He regularly performs across the Midlands and won the Ledbury Poetry Festival Slam in 2014.

Ramona Herdman's pamphlet *Bottle* is published by HappenStance Press. It was the Poetry Book Society Pamphlet

Choice for Spring 2018 and one of the Poetry School's Books of the Year 2017. She won the Poetry Society Hamish Canham prize 2017. @ramonaherdman

Maryam Hessavi is a British, Manchester-based poet of English and Iranian descent. Her poetry has been published in *Smoke Magazine* and is forthcoming in *Ambit*. She is a Ledbury Emerging Poetry Critic, with reviews featured in *The Manchester Review, Poetry London* and The Poetry School website.

Nicola Jackson writes in London and Cumbria, inspired by landscape and ancient communities. Her poetry is published in journals and newspapers. She has won prizes including the Geoff Stevens Memorial Prize 2017 for her debut collection, *Difficult Women*, (Indigo Dreams Press). She has an MA in Writing Poetry.

Angela Kirby was born in rural Lancashire when there was a strong tradition of festivals, cultural and religious. She now lives in London. Shoestring Press published her four collection: *Mr Irresistible, Dirty Work, A Scent of Winter, The Days After Always,* and *New and Selected Poems*. A fifth is due out in 2019.

Joan Lennon lives in Fife. By day she is a novelist and has recently had her 21st book published, but by night she is a poet. Her latest pamphlet – a narrative poem called *Granny Garbage* – is published by HappenStance.

Nick Littler is a poet and songwriter based in Cardiff. His poem 'The Girls from Maynard's' appeared in the Emma Press anthology *In Transit: Poems of Travel*. He writes and records music under the name Pocket Witch, and his first album, Nothing the Sun, came out in June 2018.

Derek Littlewood is a poet and naturalist living in Worcestershire. He has collected stones from many seaside locations, including Cornwall and Lizard Point, the site of many family holidays with his wife and children.

Roy McFarlane is a former Birmingham Poet Laureate and current poet-in-residence at the Birmingham & Midland Institute. He has three collections: *Celebrate Wha?* (Smokestack, 2011), *Beginning With Your Last Breath* and *The Healing Next Time* (Nine Arches, 2016 and 2018).

Kibriya Mehrban is a University of Birmingham Creative Writing graduate whose poetry first featured in the inaugural Verve Poetry Festival anthology *This is Not Your Final Form* (Emma Press, 2017). As of 2018, she is interning at Writing West Midlands and relentlessly pursues poetry in all its forms.

Fiona Moore's first collection *The Distal Point* has just come out from HappenStance Press and is a Poetry Book Society Autumn 2018 Recommendation. She is co-editing *Magma* 72 on climate change.

Tom Moyser lives in London and is an English teacher. His poetry has been published in the First Story anthology *Footsteps*. Every August, he attends a folk music festival in Sidmouth and has been in their Torchlight Procession about three times.

Margot Myers lives in Oxford. Her poems and flash-fiction have had some success in competitions including Havant, Cinammon, and Bridport. She has been published in *The Interpreter's House*, and the Emma Press anthologies of *Dance*, *Urban Myths and Legends* and *Aunts*. She celebrates as many feasts and festivals as possible.

Carolyn O'Connell lived in London for most of her life and has recently moved to Cheshire. Her poetry has been widely published in magazines and anthologies both in the UK and US, including by *Envoi, Reach* and *Aspire*. Her first collection, *Timelines*, was published by Indigo Dreams in 2014.

Claire Orchard is a poet from Wellington, New Zealand, whose father was born and raised in Farnworth, Lancashire. Her first poetry collection, *Cold Water Cure*, was published by Victoria University Press in 2016. claireorchardpoet.com

Cheryl Pearson lives and writes in Manchester. Her poems have been published in *The Guardian, Southword, Under The Radar* and *The Interpreter's House*. She has twice been nominated for a Pushcart Prize, and is a reader for Frontier Poetry. Her first collection, *Oysterlight*, is available now from Pindrop Press.

Kathy Pimlott's pamphlet *Goose Fair Night* (Emma Press) was published in 2016. Her poems have appeared in magazines including *Poem, Magma, The North, South Bank Poetry, Morning Star* and *Brittle Star,* and in several anthologies. Kathy lives in Seven Dials, London, where she works as a public realm project manager.

D A Prince lives in Leicestershire and London. Her second collection, *Common Ground* (HappenStance Press, 2014), won the East Midlands Book Award 2015.

Kim M. Russell grew up in London in the sixties, when she enjoyed day trips to the south coast with her grandmother and sister, and one memorable holiday in Clacton with a glamorous aunt – rich pickings for a poet. She now lives in Norfolk with her husband and two cats.

Laura Seymour's first collection, *The Shark Cage*, won the 2013 Cinnamon Press debut poetry collection award and was published in 2015. Her poems have appeared in several journals including *The Poetry Review, Poetry London, Magma, Envoi, Iota, Ambit, Glitterwolf, Prole* and *Mslexia*.

Natalie Shaw lives in London and works for the Government Digital Service. Her poems can be found in many different print and online journals, as well as in a variety of anthologies.

Hollie-Anne Slatcher is from Surrey and is currently studying Creative Writing and English Literature at the University of Birmingham. 'The Queens Head At Christmas' is her first poem to be published and is based on a traditional pub in Hastings, which her grandparents used to own.

Pam Thompson is a poet, lecturer, reviewer and writing tutor based in Leicester. Her publications include *The Japan Quiz* (Redbeck Press, 2009) and *Show Date and Time*, (smith|doorstop, 2006). Pam has a PhD in Creative Writing and her second collection, *Strange Fashion*, was recently published by Pindrop Press.

Beth L. Thompson is from Liverpool, where she grew up dancing, singing, guitar-playing and writing. Beth recently completed her MA in Writing at the University of Warwick, where her work was anthologised in *Moonshine* (Ball Bearing Press, 2017). She is currently working on her first novel.

Louise Walker lives in London and has been teaching English for over 30 years in girls' schools. Her poems first appeared in the Florio Society's anthologies (Sycamore Press). In 2017 her pamphlet *An Ordinary Miracle* was published by the Barafundle Press.

Rob Walton is proud to have been born in Scunthorpe, the 'Industrial Garden Town', a few miles from where the Haxey Hood takes place. He now lives on Tyneside. His poems and short fictions have been published in various places.

Ros Woolner grew up in Bourne End, a village on the Thames between Marlow and Cookham. Her poems have appeared in *Magma*, *The Cannon's Mouth*, *Under the Radar* and a number of anthologies. Her first pamphlet, *On the Wing,* was published by Offa's Press in 2018. www.roswoolner.co.uk

ABOUT THE EMMA PRESS

small press, big dreams

☙❧

The Emma Press is an independent publisher dedicated to producing beautiful, thought-provoking books. It was founded in 2012 by Emma Dai'an Wright in Winnersh and is now based in the Jewellery Quarter in Birmingham, UK.

The Emma Press publishes themed poetry anthologies, single-author poetry and fiction chapbooks and books for children, with a growing list of translations.

Moon Juice, a poetry collection by Kate Wakeling for children aged 8+, won the 2017 CLiPPA and was also nominated for the 2018 CILIP Carnegie Medal. Having been shortlisted in both 2014 and 2015, the Emma Press won the Michael Marks Award for Poetry Pamphlet Publishers in 2016.

The Emma Press is passionate about publishing literature which is welcoming and accessible. Sign up to the Emma Press newsletter to hear about upcoming events, publications and calls for submissions.

theemmapress.com
emmavalleypress.blogspot.co.uk

Once Upon a Time in Birmingham: Women who Dared to Dream

Words by Louise Palfreyman, illustrations by Jan Bowman, Yasmin Bryan, Amy Louise Evans, Saadia Hipkiss, Chein Shyan Lee, Farah Osseili and Michelle Turton

RRP £14.99 / ISBN 978-1-910139-51-6

Who was the world's first female programmer? Who made history as the first British woman to sail solo around the world non-stop? Who is Birmingham's first female Muslim MP? Meet Mary Lee Berners-Lee, Lisa Clayton, Shabana Mahmood and many more in *Once Upon a Time in Birmingham*, a lively introduction to thirty of Birmingham's most awe-inspiring women, past and present.

Malkin

Poems by Camille Ralphs
RRP £5 / ISBN 978-1-910139-30-1

Malkin brims and bubbles with the voices of those accused in the Pendle Witch Trials of 1612. Thirteen men and women – speaking across the centuries via Ralphs' heady use of free spelling – plead, boast and confess, immersing the reader in this charged and dangerous time in history.

Goose Fair Night

Poems by Kathy Pimlott
RRP £6.50 / ISBN 978-1-910139-35-6

Goose Fair Night is a generous, jellied feast of a book, full of sharp-eyed yet tender details about friendship, family and familiarity. The poems plunge us into the Midlands, bustling central London, seaside scenes, questionable pots of jam, and the captivating worldview of Pimlott's grandmother Enid.

Homesickness and Exile:
Poems about Longing and Belonging

Edited by Rachel Piercey & Emma Dai'an Wright

RRP £10 / ISBN 978-1-910139-02-8

How does it feel to be a foreigner? Can you choose where you call home? What if you reject your home or your home rejects you? *Homesickness and Exile* is a fascinating collection of poems about the fundamental human need to belong to a place, as poets from across the world provide profound and moving insights into the emotional pull of countries and cities. Poems about homecoming, departure and both voluntary and involuntary exile provoke reflections on alienation and identity, and a recurring theme is the yearning for a sense of belonging and acceptance by a place.